Francis Frith's
Cheltenham

Photographic Memories

Francis Frith's
Cheltenham

John Bainbridge

First published in the United Kingdom in 2000 by
Frith Book Company Ltd

Hardback Edition
ISBN 1-85937-285-6

Paperback Edition
ISBN 1-85937-095-0

Reprinted in paperback 2002

Text and Design copyright © Frith Book Company Ltd
Photographs copyright © The Francis Frith Collection

The Frith photographs and the Frith logo are reproduced under licence from
Heritage Photographic Resources Ltd, the owners of the Frith archive and trademarks

All rights reserved. No photograph in this publication may be sold to a third party other than in
the original form of this publication, or framed for sale to a third party.
No parts of this publication may be reproduced, stored in a retrieval system, or
transmitted, in any form, or by any means, electronic, mechanical, photocopying, recording or
otherwise, without the prior
permission of the publishers and copyright holder.

British Library Cataloguing in Publication Data

Francis Frith's Around Cheltenham
John Bainbridge

Frith Book Company Ltd
Frith's Barn, Teffont,
Salisbury, Wiltshire SP3 5QP
Tel: +44 (0) 1722 716 376
Email: info@francisfrith.co.uk
www.francisfrith.co.uk

Printed and bound in Great Britain

As with any historical database the Frith archive is constantly being corrected and improved
and the publishers would welcome information on omissions or inaccuracies

Contents

Francis Frith: Victorian Pioneer	7
Frith's Archive - A Unique Legacy	10
Cheltenham - An Introduction	12
Streets of Fashion	16
Buildings and Gardens	50
A Seat of Learning	64
Round and About	76
Index	87
Free Mounted Print Voucher	91

Francis Frith: *Victorian Pioneer*

FRANCIS FRITH, Victorian founder of the world-famous photographic archive, was a complex and multi-talented man. A devout Quaker and a highly successful Victorian businessman, he was both philosophic by nature and pioneering in outlook.

By 1855 Francis Frith had already established a wholesale grocery business in Liverpool, and sold it for the astonishing sum of £200,000, which is the equivalent today of over £15,000,000. Now a multi-millionaire, he was able to indulge his passion for travel. As a child he had pored over travel books written by early explorers, and his fancy and imagination had been stirred by family holidays to the sublime mountain regions of Wales and Scotland. 'What a land of spirit-stirring and enriching scenes and places!' he had written. He was to return to these scenes of grandeur in later years to 'recapture the thousands of vivid and tender memories', but with a different purpose. Now in his thirties, and captivated by the new science of photography, Frith set out on a series of pioneering journeys to the Nile regions that occupied him from 1856 until 1860.

Intrigue and Adventure

He took with him on his travels a specially-designed wicker carriage that acted as both dark-room and sleeping chamber. These far-flung journeys were packed with intrigue and adventure. In his life story, written when he was sixty-three, Frith tells of being held captive by bandits, and of fighting 'an awful midnight battle to the very point of surrender with a deadly pack of hungry, wild dogs'. Sporting flowing Arab costume, Frith arrived at Akaba by camel seventy years before Lawrence, where he encountered 'desert princes and rival sheikhs, blazing with jewel-hilted swords'.

During these extraordinary adventures he was assiduously exploring the desert regions bordering the Nile and patiently recording the antiquities and peoples with his camera. He was the first photographer to venture beyond the sixth cataract. Africa was still the mysterious 'Dark Continent', and Stanley and Livingstone's historic meeting was a decade into the future. The conditions for picture taking confound belief. He laboured for hours in his wicker dark-room in the sweltering heat of the desert, while the volatile chemicals fizzed dangerously in their trays. Often he was forced to work in remote tombs and caves where conditions were cooler. Back in London he exhibited his photographs and was 'rapturously cheered' by members of the Royal Society. His reputation as a photographer was made overnight. An eminent modern historian has likened their impact on the population of the time to that on our own generation of the first photographs taken on the surface of the moon.

Venture of a Life-Time

Characteristically, Frith quickly spotted the opportunity to create a new business as a specialist publisher of photographs. He lived in an era of immense and sometimes violent change. For the poor in the early part of Victoria's reign work was a drudge and the hours long, and people had precious little free time to enjoy themselves. Most had no transport other than a cart or gig at their disposal, and had not travelled far beyond the boundaries of their own town or village. However, by the 1870s, the railways had threaded their way across the country, and Bank Holidays and half-day Saturdays had been made obligatory by Act of Parliament. All of a sudden the ordinary working man and his family were able to enjoy days out and see a little more of the world.

With characteristic business acumen, Francis Frith foresaw that these new tourists would enjoy having souvenirs to commemorate their days out. In 1860 he married Mary Ann Rosling and set out with the intention of photographing every city, town and village in Britain. For the next thirty years he travelled the country by train and by pony and trap, producing fine photographs of seaside resorts and beauty spots that were keenly bought by millions of Victorians. These prints were painstakingly pasted into family albums and pored over during the dark nights of winter, rekindling precious memories of summer excursions.

The Rise of Frith & Co

Frith's studio was soon supplying retail shops all over the country. To meet the demand he gathered about him a small team of photographers, and published the work of independent artist-photographers of the calibre of Roger Fenton and Francis Bedford. In order to gain some understanding of the scale of Frith's business one only has to look at the catalogue issued by Frith & Co in 1886: it runs to some 670 pages, listing not only many thousands of views of the British Isles but also many photographs of most European countries, and China, Japan, the USA and

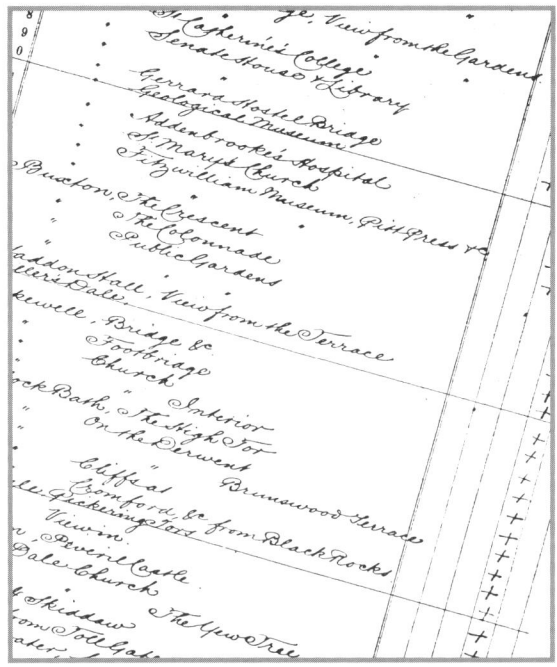

Canada – note the sample page shown above from the hand-written *Frith & Co* ledgers detailing pictures taken. By 1890 Frith had created the greatest specialist photographic publishing company in the world, with over 2,000 outlets – more than the combined number that Boots and W H Smith have today! The picture on the right shows the *Frith & Co* display board at Ingleton in the Yorkshire Dales. Beautifully constructed with mahogany frame and gilt inserts, it could display up to a dozen local scenes.

Postcard Bonanza

The ever-popular holiday postcard we know today took many years to develop. In 1870 the Post Office issued the first plain cards, with a pre-printed stamp on one face. In 1894 they allowed other publishers' cards to be sent through the mail with an attached adhesive halfpenny stamp. Demand grew rapidly, and in 1895 a new size of postcard was permitted called the court card, but there was little room for illustration. In 1899, a year after Frith's death, a new card measuring 5.5 x 3.5 inches became the standard format, but it was not until 1902 that the divided back came into being, with address and message on one face and a full-size illustration on the other. *Frith & Co* were in the vanguard of postcard development, and Frith's sons Eustace and Cyril continued their father's monumental task, expanding the number of views offered to the public and recording more and more places in Britain, as the coasts and countryside were opened up to mass travel.

Francis Frith died in 1898 at his villa in Cannes, his great project still growing. The archive he created continued in business for another seventy years. By 1970 it contained over a third of a million pictures of 7,000 cities, towns and villages. The massive photographic record Frith has left to us stands as a living monument to a special and very remarkable man.

Frith's Archive: *A Unique Legacy*

FRANCIS FRITH'S legacy to us today is of immense significance and value, for the magnificent archive of evocative photographs he created provides a unique record of change in 7,000 cities, towns and villages throughout Britain over a century and more. Frith and his fellow studio photographers revisited locations many times down the years to update their views, compiling for us an enthralling and colourful pageant of British life and character.

We tend to think of Frith's sepia views of Britain as nostalgic, for most of us use them to conjure up memories of places in our own lives with which we have family associations. It often makes us forget that to Francis Frith they were records of daily life as it was actually being lived in the cities, towns and villages of his day. The Victorian age was one of great and often bewildering change for ordinary people, and though the pictures evoke an impression of slower times, life was as busy and hectic as it is today.

We are fortunate that Frith was a photographer of the people, dedicated to recording the minutiae of everyday life. For it is this sheer wealth of visual data, the painstaking chronicle of changes in dress, transport, street layouts, buildings, housing, engineering and landscape that captivates us so much today. His remarkable images offer us a powerful link with the past and with the lives of our ancestors.

Today's Technology

Computers have now made it possible for Frith's many thousands of images to be accessed almost instantly. In the Frith archive today, each photograph is carefully 'digitised' then stored on a CD Rom. Frith archivists can locate a single photograph amongst thousands within seconds. Views can be catalogued and sorted under a variety of categories of place and content to the immediate benefit of researchers.

Inexpensive reference prints can be created for them at the touch of a mouse button, and a wide range of books and other printed materials assembled and published for a wider, more general readership - in the next twelve months over a hundred Frith local history titles will be published! The day-to-day workings of the archive are very different from how they were in Francis Frith's time: imagine the herculean task of sorting through eleven tons of glass negatives as Frith had to do to locate a particular

See Frith at www.frithbook.co.uk

sequence of pictures! Yet the archive still prides itself on maintaining the same high standards of excellence laid down by Francis Frith, including the painstaking cataloguing and indexing of every view.

It is curious to reflect on how the internet now allows researchers in America and elsewhere greater instant access to the archive than Frith himself ever enjoyed. Many thousands of individual views can be called up on screen within seconds on one of the Frith internet sites, enabling people living continents away to revisit the streets of their ancestral home town, or view places in Britain where they have enjoyed holidays. Many overseas researchers welcome the chance to view special theme selections, such as transport, sports, costume and ancient monuments.

We are certain that Francis Frith would have heartily approved of these modern developments in imaging techniques, for he himself was always working at the very limits of Victorian photographic technology.

The Value of the Archive Today

Because of the benefits brought by the computer, Frith's images are increasingly studied by social historians, by researchers into genealogy and ancestory, by architects, town planners, and by teachers and schoolchildren involved in local history projects.

In addition, the archive offers every one of us an opportunity to examine the places where we and our families have lived and worked down the years. Highly successful in Frith's own era, the archive is now, a century and more on, entering a new phase of popularity.

The Past in Tune with the Future

Historians consider the Francis Frith Collection to be of prime national importance. It is the only archive of its kind remaining in private ownership and has been valued at a million pounds. However, this figure is now rapidly increasing as digital technology enables more and more people around the world to enjoy its benefits.

Francis Frith's archive is now housed in an historic timber barn in the beautiful village of Teffont in Wiltshire. Its founder would not recognize the archive office as it is today. In place of the many thousands of dusty boxes containing glass plate negatives and an all-pervading odour of photographic chemicals, there are now ranks of computer screens. He would be amazed to watch his images travelling round the world at unimaginable speeds through network and internet lines.

The archive's future is both bright and exciting. Francis Frith, with his unshakeable belief in making photographs available to the greatest number of people, would undoubtedly approve of what is being done today with his lifetime's work. His photographs, depicting our shared past, are now bringing pleasure and enlightenment to millions around the world a century and more after his death.

Cheltenham
- An Introduction

Cheltenham adorns the borderland between the western escarpment of the Cotswolds and the broad plain of the Vale of Gloucester like some architectural jewel; it is a perfect Regency health spa, almost untouched at its heart by the unkind developments that ruined so many British towns during the 20th century.

Three centuries ago, Cheltenham was a not very distinctive country community; 'a market town in the vale', commented the Tudor topographer Leland when he called there during the reign of Henry VIII. It was a place visited mostly by shepherds with their flocks, by wool packers, and later on by stagecoaches and sundry travellers on their journey to somewhere else. Cheltenham enjoyed little fame except as a town at the back of beyond.

Yet people have lived on this site since Roman times. Saxon armies marched this way, and Anglo-Saxon kings established a religious house, perhaps not grand enough to be called a monastery, in the immediate vicinity - a building probably burnt out of existence by Danish marauders, who ravaged the fledgling community on the banks of the little River Chelt. In medieval times much of the surrounding land belonged to the church; local people earned a living from the wool trade and the growing of crops. It was around this time that the market that Leland visited was established. It is quite likely that the stone for the more substantial buildings of the town was taken from quarries in the neighbouring hills, just as the Georgian builders of the spa obtained it centuries later. But most of the everyday residences would probably have been made out of wood from the forests that were still being hewn down and pushed back at this time. The population at around the time of

Leland's visit would probably have been around a thousand.

The future spa town's first mineral spring was discovered in 1715 by a careful observer who had spent some time watching the watering habits of the local pigeons, who always seemed so fat and full of life. A pump room was constructed in 1738, and towards the end of the 18th century, King George III gave the growing town the royal seal of approval by bringing his family to take the waters. Business boomed; and when the town of Cheltenham Spa became a city, its grateful citizens incorporated a pigeon into its crest.

Clearly, the old Cheltenham could not provide either the ambience or the practical facilities to cater for its new upmarket clientele, who were beginning to grumble about the quality of the ancient inns and small boarding houses. Therefore, a calculated campaign of redesign and rebuilding was inaugurated. The hillside quarries were plundered once more for their stone, and the subsequent building boom was to give us the beautiful and elegant Cheltenham that we know today, with its wide avenues, handsome terraced houses and luxury villas.

The old line of the town had followed the ancient route that is now the High Street, but the great open spaces on either side were now incorporated into the settlement. Assembly rooms were opened so that balls and entertainments might be held to amuse the growing number of visitors, after they had spent the day taking their water treatment. Walks and formal rides were laid out for beneficial exercise, and the roads were eventually paved to allow long-gowned ladies to avoid the usual mud of the

Cheltenham c1950 C75032

thoroughfares.

Cheltenham came into its own upon receiving the patronage of the royal family. The long-drawn-out Napoleonic Wars, which closed off the Continent to wealthy visitors, brought a great influx of visitors to the spa. Several new mineral springs were opened; many had elaborate pump rooms designed to cater for the most fastidious of tastes. In the aftermath of the war, the town began to spread across what had been green fields and open common land as its citizens attempted to absorb this increased number of patrons. Cheltenham's population grew substantially at this time: many visitors who had fallen for its charms decided to settle here.

The 19th century saw the town expand as retired empire-builders, colonial civil servants and pensioned military officers sought refuge after a lifetime in warmer climes. Not everyone was impressed. The social commentator William Cobbett in his book 'Rural Rides' considered Cheltenham to be a 'nasty ill-looking place', full of 'East India plunderers, West Indian floggers, English tax-gorgers, gluttons, drunkards and debauchers of all descriptions, female as well as male'. Cobbett hurried on to critically examine other places. His judgement may seem harsh, but all fashionable resorts at that time probably attracted an equal measure of exploiters and hangers-on, given the rich pickings that were to be had.

Evidence suggests that Victorian Cheltenham was a calmer place. New streets were laid out, houses built and churches founded. The importance of the town began to depend as much on the fortunes of its residents as on its

Cheltenham, The Boating Lake 1901 47297

visitors. This was particularly the case with the development of Cheltenham as a renowned seat of learning. The first colleges, founded early in the Queen's reign, were private concerns, effectively companies, with the shareholders entitled to nominate pupils. Many of the original boys were the sons of army officers, and their education was designed to equip them for a future career in the services. By the middle of the 19th century, the colleges had acquired considerable reputations throughout the British Empire, so much so that families in far-flung corners of the Empire were starting to send their children across the waters to gain a Cheltenham education.

Cheltenham Ladies College came into existence to cater for the daughters of the newly affluent middle-class, who to a certain extent were being communally educated for the first time. Headmistresses such as the pioneering Miss Dorothea Beale took up the challenge, providing a real and substantial education, very different from the simpler acquirements of the earlier girls' boarding academies or the skills passed on by governesses and private tutors. Miss Beale believed that girls should be able to compete with boys, at least academically. She saw her college as a preparation for a university education, and added to Cheltenham's reputation by making it a groundbreaking centre for the proper education of women. A number of her pupils went on to achieve entry to the women's colleges that were opening at Oxford and Cambridge.

The presence of these educational establishments gave Cheltenham the atmosphere of a university town, though there has always been a local debate as to whether or not the architectural merits of the college buildings match that of the standard of education.

In the last century, Cheltenham became a busy city, with modern industries, world-famous music and literature festivals, and a National Hunt racecourse - home of the Cheltenham Gold Cup. Despite the reduction of the city's importance as a spa, Cheltenham has continued to attract tourists, who find the place an admirable touring centre for the Cotswolds and the Vale of Gloucester. Much of the Georgian and Regency heart of the old town has remained intact; for developments and industries have tended to ring the town rather than invade its old centre.

The Frith photographers captured these scenes of Cheltenham at a perfect time, before its streets became too cluttered with the intrusive presence of the motor car, and with the old spa town relatively intact and not so very different in appearance from the health resort so loved by earlier generations of visitors.

Cheltenham, The Promenade 1923 73471

Streets of Fashion

In this first sequence of photographs, we get a good idea of how Cheltenham changed from a small country town to a leading spa and health resort. It is interesting to compare the views of the Promenade, purposely designed for Cheltenham's newer role, with the photographs that follow of the High Street. The latter is narrow in comparison with the Promenade, its road space given over to the passage of vehicles rather than of pedestrians. The opposite is true with the design of the Promenade; here the pavements are much wider than the roads, allowing residents and visitors to walk in safety away from traffic, which was contained in narrow carriageways. Similarly, the buildings in avenues such as the Promenade are much more spacious and elegant than the original dwellings and lodging places in the High Street.

The Promenade Drive c1875 C75501
Three centuries ago, Cheltenham was another stone village on the edge of the Cotswolds. Its fortunes changed in 1715 when a mineral spring was discovered. Within a few years, fashionable society had begun to arrive to take the waters.

▼ **The Promenade 1901** 47260
Not every visitor was impressed by the elegance of Cheltenham Spa. William Cobbett described the town as a 'nasty ill-looking place', full of 'East India plunderers, West Indian floggers, English tax-gorgers...gluttons, drunkards and debauchers of all descriptions, female as well as male'.

▼ **Upper Promenade 1901** 47263
Cheltenham's long Promenade, with its stylish buildings, became one of the town's most fashionable residential areas when the spa town began to spread away from the vicinity of the High Street and the old town.

▲ **The Promenade 1901**
47261
Cheltenham soon became a retirement home for military officers and colonial administrators who occupied the spreading Regency terraces, such as the ones seen here along the Promenade. Others lived in purpose-built villas elsewhere in the town.

Streets of Fashion

◀ **Upper Promenade 1901**
47264
Since Victorian times, Cheltenham has served as a venue for national meetings and conferences, thanks to the many halls available in the town. Here we see a carriage waiting outside a conference of the British Medical Association.

The Promenade 1907 59032
Before the Promenade was built, this wooded area was known as Sherborne Walks - a favourite venue for promenading early visitors. The long-gone Sherborne Pump Room was then the only building of note to be seen.

The Promenade 1907 59033
The population of Cheltenham grew from three thousand in 1801 to over thirteen thousand just twenty years later; this was a sure sign of Cheltenham's success as a spa town and residential centre. Cheltenham has remained a very green city, with many trees, shrubs and flowerbeds.

Streets of Fashion

The War Memorial 1907 59035
Cheltenham has always had strong connections with the military, and has thus paid the price in times of war. This Boer War Memorial, with its impressive statue of a soldier in prayer, is situated in one of the gardens of the Promenade. Most of the Cheltenham soldiers named here died in South Africa of disease rather than in battle.

Streets of Fashion

The Promenade 1923
73472
A spa town demanded that pedestrians should have priority over vehicles of any sort. The specially-designed layout of the Promenade achieved just that. The pavements and walkways are very wide, and the roads are correspondingly narrow. It is interesting to compare this designed area with the High Street, which simply evolved as a thoroughfare for stagecoaches.

◀ **The Promenade 1923**
73474
Cheltenham today has a thriving musical and literary festival, and many other connections with the arts. One of the town's most famous sons was Gustav Holst, born in 1874, a pupil at Cheltenham Grammar School. Holst composed music inspired by the local scenery long before he became famous for 'The Planets' and 'Egdon Heath'.

Streets of Fashion

◀ **The Promenade 1923**
73473
During the great building boom that followed Cheltenham's development from the 19th century onwards, much of the earlier medieval settlement was overwhelmed. St Mary's Church, the oldest in the town, is Norman in origin, and probably stands on the site of an earlier Saxon building.

▼ **The Promenade 1923**
73475
It was for the building of the Promenade and the surrounding crescents and terraces that many of the quarries were opened in the neighbouring hills. The wide streets could almost have been tailor-made for the demands of the motor car age.

◀ **The Promenade 1923**
73476
It is possible to work out the dates of Cheltenham's terraces by comparing the architectural styles. The early terraces, such as Royal Crescent, lacked the adornment of some of the later buildings; they have iron railings around their balconies instead of stone archways and colonnades.

The Promenade 1923 73478
The Sherborne Walks had a section known as the Promenade, even before the extensive building work took place. Generations of visitors and Cheltenham folk have enjoyed a stroll in this area on pleasant days.

Streets of Fashion

The Promenade 1923 73481
A chauffeur paces up and down beside his parked car, no doubt waiting for his employer to emerge from the post office or bank. The majority of well-heeled locals had servants until well into the 20th century.

The Wilson Memorial 1923 73482
Dr Edward Wilson, polar explorer and scientist, perished whilst making the homeward journey from the South Pole with Captain Scott in 1912. This fine memorial was erected a few years later.

◀ **The Promenade 1931**
83806
Cheltenham acquired a reputation as a high-quality shopping centre towards the end of Queen Victoria's reign. By the 20th century, a trip to the shops lining the eastern side of the Promenade was on every visitor's itinerary.

Streets of Fashion

◀ **The Promenade 1931** 83804
By the 1930s, the influence of the retired Anglo-Indian military officers and colonial administrators had begun to decline, and more ordinary people came to live in Cheltenham. In 1931, the population exceeded 40,000.

▶ **The Promenade, Fashion 1931**
83807v (extract from photograph overleaf)

▶ **The Promenade, Fashion 1931** 83807x
(extract from photograph overleaf)
For a long time decorum demanded that one was well-dressed for a stroll along the Promenade - even as recently as the 1930s. Casual dress was reserved for home wear, or for days out in the countryside.
Cheltenham's dress code has relaxed considerably in recent decades.

Streets of Fashion

The Promenade 1931
83807
Seen in the context of the Promenade, we can observe that everyone surrounding the pedestrians in the last two photographs was well dressed. One difference with today's strollers and shoppers would be the disappearance of headgear in the modern age. Until the 1950s it was quite usual to see nearly everyone wearing a hat of some description when walking through the streets of Cheltenham.

The Promenade 1931 83808
Much of the employment in Victorian Cheltenham had been directly related to the activities of a spa town, with a large proportion of the working population being domestic servants or employed in hotels, shops and catering facilities. By the 1930s a number of light manufacturing industries had arrived in Cheltenham offering alternative employment.

The Memorial Gardens 1937 87922
Cheltenham absorbed the industries of the last century quite well; most of the factories were sited on the outskirts of the town. Industries that have thrived have included aircraft manufacture, coachbuilding, printing and the production of porcelain ware.

Streets of Fashion

The Entrance to the Promenade 1937 87926
Even in the harsh economic climate of the 1930s, the shops of Cheltenham thrived, offering regular employment to a great many people. During the Second World War, an administrative and technical section of the United States Army was based in the town, bringing a new spirit of internationalism to Cheltenham.

The Promenade c1945 C75014
The age of popular motoring led to increased numbers of tourists coming to Cheltenham. Some came to watch events such as the Cheltenham Gold Cup at the racecourse, others to the very successful literary and musical festivals held in the town.

The Promenade c1950 C75020x
Cheltenham, like so many places in Britain, had difficulty coping with increased numbers of motor cars, given that car parks were not part of the original design. The wide avenues of the Promenade helped for a while, but in time the now-familiar car parks had to be introduced.

Streets of Fashion

The Promenade c1960 C75154
Cheltenham's skyline had changed little between the great period of the Regency and the dawn of the 1960s. In the years that followed, some high office blocks were allowed in the town centre - to the dismay of all who cared for the old spa town.

The Promenade Fountains 1923 73485
The Neptune Fountain has adorned the top end of the Promenade since 1893, when it was built as part of a project to improve the ambience of this long avenue.

The Neptune Fountain 1912 65100
Cheltenham's Borough Surveyor, Mr Hall, undertook the design of the fountain, and had the new fountain made from Portland Stone; he was supposedly inspired by Rome's Trevi Fountain.

Streets of Fashion

The Fountains 1937 87921
Cheltenham's Neptune Fountain has long been a place to linger and relax on sunny days. Before the construction of the fountain, this area was much used for street entertainments.

High Street 1901 47266
The road from London leads naturally into Cheltenham's High Street, which is one of the original thoroughfares of the town. In 1901, this urban scene was still dominated by horse-drawn vehicles and cyclists.

Streets of Fashion

High Street 1901
47265
This atmospheric photograph of the High Street shows a scene relatively unchanged since earlier Victorian days. But how much has really changed since then? The clothes may be different, and the transport is drawn by horses, but local people may still gather outside Stead and Simpson's during their summer sale.

Streets of Fashion

High Street 1906
54320
It is along this street that the Tudor topographer Leland would have been travelling when he described Cheltenham as 'a longe towne havynge a market'. At the time of Leland's visit, Cheltenham would have prospered from the sale of wool and agricultural produce.

◀ **Lower High Street c1955** C75109
Regency society eventually found lodgings in the High Street to be too modest for their social requirements. Powers were sought in Parliament to establish new residential areas, and many of the squares and avenues of modern-day Cheltenham date back to that period.

Streets of Fashion

◄ **High Street 1906**
54319
A tram takes Edwardians to Charlton Kings along a High Street decorated with some lovely examples of shop advertising signs. Potential customers are invited to buy 'Public Benefit Boots' at one shop, and the ubiquitous Singer Sewing Machine at another.

▼ **Lower High Street c1955** C75108
However, the remnants of earlier Georgian homes, taverns and inns can still be seen in and around the High Street. Walking further afield, the town explorer can see the later Regency and Victorian developments.

◄ **The Centre 1937** 87925
The Napoleonic Wars meant that the wealthiest members of Regency society could no longer visit the Continent. Many of the elite made their way to Cheltenham as an alternative to foreign travel.

The Strand 1937 87923
By the 1930s, many of the familiar chain stores had established themselves in Cheltenham - including Freeman, Hardy and Willis, seen here. Next door is Gillhams, the 'Look Round' shop.

The Centre and the Promenade c1955 C75007
The arrival of motor traffic in Cheltenham meant that road layouts had to be redesigned to facilitate the safe movement of cars and lorries. As we can see here, Cheltenham's planners made considerable efforts to make even traffic islands things of beauty.

The Centre c1960 C75129
This view of the town centre shows that many long-established trading names were thriving in Cheltenham in the middle of the last century. The roads were still coping very well with the demands of motor traffic.

The King Edward VII Statue 1923 73490
This statue of Edward VII and a child was erected by public subscription four years after the King's death. It is considered to be one of the best and most human statues of the monarch who gave his name to a peaceful era of British history.

London Road 1906
54321
Horse-drawn conveyances were mostly replaced by electric trams, which covered the major routes in and out of town; there was even a tram that regularly undertook the steep climb up towards Cleeve Hill. The tramway system was dismantled in the middle of the last century.

Lansdown Road 1901 47267
A small boy watches the Frith photographer capture this scene of Lansdown Road in the first year of Edward VII's reign. He may well have been a pupil at the nearby Dean Close School.

Lansdown Place 1923 73501
The Jearrads, those well-known local architects, designed much of the architecture in the Lansdown district. The streets of 'new' Cheltenham were much wider than those in the older part of town.

Streets of Fashion

Leckhampton Road 1923 73502
From Victorian times onwards, residential suburbs grew up on the outskirts of Cheltenham, catering for the growing number of workers in the area. Notice the tramline along the centre of the road.

Francis Frith's Cheltenham

Buildings and Gardens

Great care was taken to keep wide and open spaces in the growing health spa of Cheltenham. Many of the fine buildings and gardens shown in the following photographs were built or laid out in the 19th century, a time when other towns and cities had been taken over by the very worst effects of the Industrial Age: slums, overcrowding and disease. Despite the pressures from developers in the last century, Cheltenham has remained a green and open city - a lovely place for a stroll on dry days.

Christ Church 1906 54339
The building of Christ Church was started in 1837, under the guidance of Francis Close, who laid the foundation stone. Its Gothic Revival tower is a prominent landmark when seen from many parts of Cheltenham and the hills beyond.

▼ **Montpellier Street 1901** 47293
Designed by the well-known Cheltenham architect J N Papworth, the Montpellier Colonnade and Rotunda dominate Montpellier Street. Many of the other buildings adjoining this old spa are also the work of the former architect to the King of Wurttemburg. The Rotunda was built in 1825, behind the existing Montpellier pump room.

▼ **The Town Hall 1923** 73488
Cheltenham's Town Hall was built in the fashionable Baroque style during the reign of Edward VII. Local people have debated ever since whether its architectural appearance adds or detracts from the beauty of Cheltenham.

▲ **The Queen's Hotel 1901** 47269
The Queen's Hotel has dominated the southern end of the Promenade ever since it was built in 1837. An increase in the number of wealthy visitors to the spa meant that the old inns and small hotels could no longer cope. This hotel was opened in the first year of Victoria's reign, and was named in her honour.

Buildings and Gardens

◀ **The Queen's Hotel 1923**
73492
This classically-influenced hotel, built in the Palladian style - though an extra storey compromises the concept - was designed by the well-known Cheltenham architects R W and C Jearrad.

The Queen's Hotel 1923 73491
Many important visitors to Cheltenham stayed at the Queen's Hotel, including European royals and public figures such as Charles Dickens. The hotel adapted well to the demands of the 20th century visitor: its Victorian standards were not allowed to slip.

The Winter Gardens 1923 73495
Looking away from the Queen's Hotel, we can see one of Cheltenham's grandest open spaces. In the foreground are cannons captured from the Russians at the siege of Sebastopol. These impressive pieces of artillery were presented to the town after the Crimean War.

Buildings and Gardens

The Winter Gardens 1901 47258
As an all-the-year-round health resort, Cheltenham was required to provide facilities for entertainments in bad weather as well as good.

The Winter Gardens 1912 65099
The glass canopy of the Winter Gardens owed much to the inspiration of Paxton's Crystal Palace. The Imperial Gardens have now been laid out on this site.

◀ **Pittville Spa 1901**
47295
Cheltenham entrepreneur Joseph Pitt benefited from an Act of Parliament that enclosed common land on the northern edge of the town. Pitt took advantage of these enclosures to develop the area, which became known as Pittville. His original intention was to found an entirely new town, but financial problems prevented his ambitious plans.

Buildings and Gardens

◄ **Imperial Gardens c1955** C75060
The Imperial Gardens were laid out in the mid 20th century around the site of the old Victorian Winter Gardens - an attractive green space in the centre of Cheltenham.

▼ **Pittville Gardens 1923** 73511
Pittville's Pump Room was completed in 1830, but it never really prospered, despite the patronage of the Duke of Wellington. The building was purchased by Cheltenham Corporation in 1889; in recent years it has served the community as a venue for arts events and as the architectural section of the Gloucestershire College of Arts.

◄ **Pittville Gardens 1923** 73512
Although Pitt's grandiose plans for this area never materialised, much of the parkland and the ornamental lakes remain. This area is now a favourite place for a stroll for locals and visitors alike, who relish the quiet beauty, attractive plants and the birds.

Pittville Park, the Boating Lake 1931 83818
One favourite way to spend a few hours in Cheltenham is to hire a boat on the park lake. Water from the River Swilgate was used to create this idyllic stretch of open water.

Buildings and Gardens

Sandford Park, The Entrance 1931 83810
The rapid development of Cheltenham from old town to modern city led to the creation of many delightful open spaces in the heart of the urban community. Sandford Park has remained popular for people out for a stroll.

Sandford Park, The Pergola 1931 83812
Cheltenham owes a great deal to its team of municipal gardeners for they way they manage to keep the city colourful with flowers and shrubs during all the seasons of the year. The Pergola offers shade to pedestrians seeking to rest for a while on the many benches.

Buildings and Gardens

Sandford Park, The Waterfalls 1931 83816
There are few more lovely sounds in nature than that of running water. Where nature failed to provide waterfalls to achieve the effect, Cheltenham's designers obliged.

◄ **The Racecourse 1931**
83821
Cheltenham Racecourse is now the home of National Hunt steeplechasing in Britain; its sporting events are often patronised by members of the Royal Family and world-class jockeys and trainers.

Buildings and Gardens

◀ **The Racecourse 1931** 83820
Horseracing at Cheltenham was encouraged by the fashionable society that descended upon the spa town. The popularity of the famous three-day meets and the Cheltenham Gold Cup developed in the years between the two World Wars.

▶ **Ambrose Street and St Gregory's Catholic Church c1955** C75080
St Gregory's is one of Cheltenham's mid-Victorian churches, designed by Charles Hansom and opened in 1857. The eye-catching tower and spire was finished two years later. An earlier Regency church once occupied the same site.

▶ **St Paul's Hospital c1965** C75130
Many of Cheltenham's present residents were probably born in St Paul's Hospital. It is interesting to note the care with which its architects designed this building - a happy addition to a district of fine architecture.

A Seat of Learning

In the past two centuries Cheltenham has become a byword for the excellent quality of its public school education. The buildings of the two major colleges and the several smaller schools are spread around the city, and are fine examples of Victorian architecture - though they are not without their critics. The academic atmosphere is rather like that of a university town, and pupils from one establishment or another are a familiar sight on the city streets. Even in our modern age, Cheltenham's public schools continue to thrive, much as they have done since the Boys' College was founded in 1841.

The Boys' College 1906 54326
Cheltenham College was originally a private concern, with shareholders who were able to nominate potential pupils. Many of the early pupils were the sons of army officers, who intended to graduate into a military career. Cheltenham's reputation as an educational centre really started in 1841 with the establishment of the Boys' College. By this period, Cheltenham had already become a much-frequented spa town in which many Victorians had taken up permanent residence.

The College Library 1906 54329
By the 1860s, there were over six hundred pupils at the college, making it a worthy competitor to the older public schools such as Winchester, Eton and Rugby. This library was originally the college chapel.

The College Chapel 1906 54330
There was early criticism of the architecture of some of the college buildings. To mark the establishment's jubilee, this new chapel designed by H A Prothero was built - to great critical acclaim. Earlier college students had worshipped at Christ Church in the town.

A Seat of Learning

The College Playing Fields 1907 59039
Even today, the college boasts an annual summer cricket festival in the best public school tradition. Apart from the clothes worn by the spectators, the scenes in this sequence could have been photographed at any time during the following century. These views (see also overleaf) from the playing fields show the range of architectural styles adopted by the builders of the Victorian College.

A Seat of Learning

**The College
Playing Fields
1907** 59038

◀ **The College Museum 1907** 59044
Early exhibits at the museum included, according to the museum catalogue, 'skins of grass snakes, some flint implements, a bandolier, a Mauser carbine, a flag, a Boer hat, three stuffed bears, two stuffed heads of elk, four cases of birds, an elephant's foot, a human skull, a grasshopper in a bottle and some Indian coins'.

A Seat of Learning

◀ **The College Museum 1907** 59043
Cheltenham College Museum was converted from an old racquets court in 1870 at a cost of £700. It aimed at arousing in the pupils an interest 'in the study of science and natural history'. This important collection was finally dispersed in 1976, and many of the exhibits were sent to the Merseyside Museum.

▼ **The Gentlemen's College 1923** 73504
This original part of Cheltenham College was built in the early 1840s. Before these buildings could be occupied, classes were held in terraced houses in Bayshill, elsewhere in the town.

◀ **The Ladies' College 1901** 47275
The famous Cheltenham Ladies' College began its life at Cambray House, relocating to the present site in the 1870s. In the years that followed, pupil numbers increased and a range of new buildings began to sprawl up the hillside towards Montpellier.

The Ladies' College 1906 54324
Before Cheltenham Ladies' College was founded, there was little real education for women. Most middle-class girls were educated either at home or at boarding academies where the standard of education was not necessarily very high. Cheltenham was to become a byword for the proper education of women.

The Ladies' College, South Side 1912 65105
Much of the credit for the success of Cheltenham Ladies' College must go to the indomitable headmistress Miss Dorothea Beale, who arrived at the college in 1858 and remained in charge until her death in 1906.

A Seat of Learning

The Ladies' College 1923 73506a
Since Miss Beale's time, students have come from all over the world to study at the famous Cheltenham Ladies' College. Every visitor to the town should make a point of admiring the college buildings - if only from the outside.

▼ **The Ladies' College, Main Hall 1912** 65107

▼ **Dean Close School 1901** 47278
A new public school opened at the western fringes of Cheltenham in 1886. It was named Dean Close in honour of Francis Close, sometime Bishop of Carlisle. During his years at Cheltenham, Close had founded Christ Church and had been a leading light in the development of educational establishments around the town.

▲ **The Ladies' College, Main Hall 1912** 65108
Miss Beale was a great campaigner for university education for women, and had a vision of the Ladies' College as a preparation for this. Even today, the college has much of the atmosphere of a very select university college.

A Seat of Learning

◀ **The Junior School 1907**
59041
Pupils still sat at long rows of wooden forms in some of Cheltenham's schools until well into the last century. Many Cheltenham pupils went on to great things, often looking back with fondness at the time they spent in the town's seats of learning.

Round and About

Cheltenham is popularly claimed to be a true Cotswold town, though it lies to the west of the Cotswold escarpment. Others suggest that it is a true town of the Vale of Gloucester, lying as it does not far from the River Severn. The countryside around the spa town is certainly some of the most beautiful in England; it is a landscape of rolling downland, broad pastoral plains, quiet footpaths and ancient villages with historic churches and welcome inns. The first-time visitor should seek public transport to nearby Cleeve Hill and begin an exploration there, after admiring the views over the surrounding area. Ideally, this land is best investigated on foot, or perhaps on horseback or cycle, for delightful hidden corners may be missed if you rush through in a motor vehicle. Cheltenham is indeed fortunate in having this picturesque landscape as its back garden.

Birdlip, The George Hotel 1907 59062
A few miles south of Cheltenham lies Birdlip, surrounded by wonderful open countryside of beech woods and ancient footpaths. The George Hotel, with its famous pleasure gardens, was a favourite day out for Cheltenham's Edwardian visitors, who would arrive in either carriages such as this one or early motor vehicles.

Birdlip, The Royal George Hotel c1955 B99001
It is half a century after photograph No 59062, and the George has changed very little. A comparison with No 59062 shows only that the road has been adapted for increased motor traffic, and that the old inn carries newly-painted signs and an endorsement by the Royal Automobile Club.

Birdlip, The Hill c1955 B99011
This broad highway winds downhill from the Royal George, offering fine views over the Vale of Gloucester and the southern Cotswolds. Caravanning was to be one of the most popular ways of exploring Britain's countryside in the 1950s.

Round and About

Bishop's Cleeve, The Village c1955 B531002
Bishop's Cleeve has now become something of a small town, a dormitory for nearby Cheltenham. Nevertheless, it still has an attractive setting not far from the beauty spot of Cleeve Hill. Bishop's Cleeve church dates back to Norman times, though much of what we see today is 17th-century.

Bishop's Cleeve, Priory Lane c1960 B531006
Despite a great deal of demolition in the 1950s, Bishop's Cleeve boasts many fine old buildings. A village existed here in Saxon times, and records show that King Alfred gave land for a church here in the 8th century.

◀ **Brockworth, The Church and Brockworth Court c1960** B837002
This photograph demonstrates very clearly the relationship between church and manor house in earlier times. This was not just a matter of proximity; local gentry would have priority where church matters were concerned, with their own reserved family pews and very often the power to appoint the vicar.

◀ **Brockworth, Cooper's Hill 1907** 59070
Brockworth is situated on the Ermine Way, that ancient route that runs here between Cheltenham and Cirencester. Despite increased traffic, this remains a relatively unspoiled and attractive stretch of pastoral countryside once the houses are left behind.

▼ **Charlton Kings, A Glimpse from Charlyon Hill c1955**
C445004
When Cheltenham was undergoing its reconstruction during the 18th century, much of the stone was brought down from quarries scattered around the high ground surrounding Charlton Kings. Nature has healed many of these industrial scars, leaving only a peaceful if windswept landscape.

◀ **Charlton Kings, Cirencester Road c1955** C445001
In the 17th century, Charlton Kings was very much an agricultural district, not at all the suburb of Cheltenham it is today. It was once famous for tobacco production. James I, who hated what he called the 'noxious weed', issued warrants for the destruction of the crop. Not surprisingly, the local tobacco industry declined in the face of this royal displeasure.

The Devil's Chimney 1901 47256
This tall limestone pillar stands above the quarries on Leckhampton Hill. The strangely-shaped and eroded rock is a relic of the quarrying industry that provided much of the stone for the growing town of Cheltenham. From here, there are extensive views across the plains surrounding the River Severn and as far north as the Malvern Hills.

The Devil's Chimney 1901 47257
The Devil's Chimney has been a favourite subject since the earliest days of photography. The Chimney remains a favourite location for the publisher of picture postcards today.

Round and About

Cleeve Hill, Wash Pool Farm 1907 59060
Cleeve Hill is a distinctive and windswept plateau, surrounded by ancient farms and pretty hamlets. Much of this area has been common land from medieval times, and some local cottagers retain the right to graze animals and gather fuel.

▼ Hucclecote, The Village c1965 H337004

Many visitors to Cheltenham will recognise this scene, for it remains a well-known approach road to Cheltenham. However, if the car is left behind and the area explored on foot, much of Hucclecote's original village identity can still be discovered.

▼ Deerhurst, The Saxon Church 1901 47306

Deerhurst adorns the Vale of Gloucester in a lovely setting between the towns of Tewkesbury and Cheltenham. Its church is Saxon, with later additions, and was probably founded when the first Anglo-Saxon settlers established their tiny farms in what had been a Celtic heartland.

▲ Colesbourne, Lower Hilcot c1960 C453010

An ancient ford and footbridge, an abandoned cartwheel and the splash of water running over a tiny weir - this delightful photograph of stone cottages and attractive gardens reminds us that the countryside maintained a timeless air, even in the hurry of the 20th century.

Round and About

◀ **Prestbury, The Village 1907** 59051
Prestbury, not far from Cheltenham Racecourse, has the reputation of being one of the most haunted villages in England. A spectral cavalier hurries through its streets, a monk haunts its shady corners, and a violent phantom hovers to trap the unwary. Prestbury remains a pleasant place for a stroll - though go in daylight if you are of a nervous disposition.

Prestbury, High Street c1955 P112015
By the 1950s, the tramlines had disappeared, and motor vehicles replaced the cyclists of earlier days on this route to the beauty spot of Cleeve Hill. See how some of the cottages in the earlier photograph have been transformed into shops to cater for the increase in tourism.

Staverton, The Church 1896 38240
The M5 motorway divides this village and its surrounding countryside from Cheltenham. In earlier days, Staverton's agricultural products would have been supplied to the growing town, and its lanes would have been well-ridden by horse owners visiting the neighbouring spa.

Index

Ambrose Street 63
Boating Lake 14
Boy's College 64-65
Centre 15, 43, 44, 45
Christ Church 50-51
College 66, 67, 68-69, 70-71
Dean Close School 74
Gentlemen's College 71
High Street 37, 38-39, 40-41, 42-43
Imperial Gardens 56-57
Junior School 75
King Edward VII Statue 45
Ladies' College 71, 72, 73, 74-75
Lansdown Place 48
Lansdown Road 48
Leckhampton Road 49
London Road 46-47
Lower High Street 42, 43
Memorial Gardens 32
Montpellier Street 52
Neptune Fountain 35, 36
Pittville Gardens 57
Pittville Park 58
Pittville Spa 56
Promenade 15, 16-17, 18-19, 20, 22-23, 24-25, 26, 27, 28-29, 30-31, 32, 33, 34, 35, 44
Queen's Hotel 52-53, 54
Racecourse 62-63
Sandford Park 59, 60-61
St Gregory's Church 63
St Paul's Hospital 63
Strand 44
Town Hall 52
War Memorial 21
Wilson Memorial 27
Winter Gardens 54, 55

Round and About

Birdlip 76-77, 78
Bishop's Cleeve 79
Brockworth 80-81
Charlton Kings 81
Cleeve Hill 83
Colesbourne 84-85
Deerhurst 84
Devil's Chimney 82
Hucclecote 84
Prestbury 85, 86
Staverton 86

Frith Book Co Titles

www.frithbook.co.uk

The Frith Book Company publishes over 100 new titles each year. A selection of those currently available are listed below. For latest catalogue please contact Frith Book Co.

Town Books 96pp, 100 photos. County and Themed Books 128pp, 150 photos (unless specified). All titles hardback laminated case and jacket except those indicated pb (paperback)

Title	ISBN	Price
Around Bakewell	1-85937-113-2	£12.99
Around Barnstaple	1-85937-084-5	£12.99
Around Bath	1-85937-097-7	£12.99
Berkshire (pb)	1-85937-191-4	£9.99
Around Blackpool	1-85937-049-7	£12.99
Around Bognor Regis	1-85937-055-1	£12.99
Around Bournemouth	1-85937-067-5	£12.99
Brighton (pb)	1-85937-192-2	£8.99
British Life A Century Ago	1-85937-103-5	£17.99
Buckinghamshire (pb)	1-85937-200-7	£9.99
Around Cambridge	1-85937-092-6	£12.99
Cambridgeshire	1-85937-086-1	£14.99
Canals and Waterways	1-85937-129-9	£17.99
Cheshire	1-85937-045-4	£14.99
Around Chester	1-85937-090-x	£12.99
Around Chichester	1-85937-089-6	£12.99
Churches of Berkshire	1-85937-170-1	£17.99
Churches of Dorset	1-85937-172-8	£17.99
Colchester (pb)	1-85937-188-4	£8.99
Cornwall	1-85937-054-3	£14.99
Cumbria	1-85937-101-9	£14.99
Dartmoor	1-85937-145-0	£14.99
Around Derby	1-85937-046-2	£12.99
Derbyshire (pb)	1-85937-196-5	£9.99
Devon	1-85937-052-7	£14.99
Dorset	1-85937-075-6	£14.99
Dorset Coast	1-85937-062-4	£14.99
Down the Severn	1-85937-118-3	£14.99
Down the Thames	1-85937-121-3	£14.99
Around Dublin	1-85937-058-6	£12.99
East Sussex	1-85937-130-2	£14.99
Around Eastbourne	1-85937-061-6	£12.99
Edinburgh (pb)	1-85937-193-0	£8.99
English Castles	1-85937-078-0	£14.99
Essex	1-85937-082-9	£14.99
Around Exeter	1-85937-126-4	£12.99
Exmoor	1-85937-132-9	£14.99
Around Falmouth	1-85937-066-7	£12.99
Around Great Yarmouth	1-85937-085-3	£12.99
Around Guildford	1-85937-117-5	£12.99
Hampshire	1-85937-064-0	£14.99
Around Harrogate	1-85937-112-4	£12.99
Around Horsham	1-85937-127-2	£12.99
Around Ipswich	1-85937-133-7	£12.99
Ireland (pb)	1-85937-181-7	£9.99
Isle of Man	1-85937-065-9	£14.99
Isle of Wight	1-85937-114-0	£14.99
Kent (pb)	1-85937-189-2	£9.99
Around Leicester	1-85937-073-x	£12.99
Leicestershire (pb)	1-85937-185-x	£9.99
Around Lincoln	1-85937-111-6	£12.99
Lincolnshire	1-85937-135-3	£14.99
London (pb)	1-85937-183-3	£9.99
Around Maidstone	1-85937-056-x	£12.99
New Forest	1-85937-128-0	£14.99
Around Newark	1-85937-105-1	£12.99
Around Newquay	1-85937-140-x	£12.99
North Devon Coast	1-85937-146-9	£14.99
Northumberland and Tyne & Wear	1-85937-072-1	£14.99
Norwich (pb)	1-85937-194-9	£8.99
Around Nottingham	1-85937-060-8	£12.99
Nottinghamshire (pb)	1-85937-187-6	£9.99
Around Oxford	1-85937-096-9	£12.99
Oxfordshire	1-85937-076-4	£14.99
Peak District	1-85937-100-0	£14.99
Around Penzance	1-85937-069-1	£12.99
Around Plymouth	1-85937-119-1	£12.99
Around St Ives	1-85937-068-3	£12.99
Around Scarborough	1-85937-104-3	£12.99
Scotland (pb)	1-85937-182-5	£9.99
Scottish Castles	1-85937-077-2	£14.99
Around Sevenoaks and Tonbridge	1-85937-057-8	£12.99
Around Southampton	1-85937-088-8	£12.99
Around Southport	1-85937-106-x	£12.99

Available from your local bookshop or from the publisher

Frith Book Co Titles (continued)

Title	ISBN	Price
Around Shrewsbury	1-85937-110-8	£12.99
Shropshire	1-85937-083-7	£14.99
South Devon Coast	1-85937-107-8	£14.99
South Devon Living Memories	1-85937-168-x	£14.99
Staffordshire (96pp)	1-85937-047-0	£12.99
Stone Circles & Ancient Monuments	1-85937-143-4	£17.99
Around Stratford upon Avon	1-85937-098-5	£12.99
Sussex (pb)	1-85937-184-1	£9.99
Around Torbay	1-85937-063-2	£12.99
Around Truro	1-85937-147-7	£12.99
Victorian & Edwardian Kent	1-85937-149-3	£14.99
Victorian & Edwardian Yorkshire	1-85937-154-x	£14.99
Warwickshire (pb)	1-85937-203-1	£9.99
Welsh Castles	1-85937-120-5	£14.99
West Midlands	1-85937-109-4	£14.99
West Sussex	1-85937-148-5	£14.99
Wiltshire	1-85937-053-5	£14.99
Around Winchester	1-85937-139-6	£12.99

Frith Book Co titles available Autumn 2000

Title	ISBN	Price	Month
Croydon Living Memories (pb)	1-85937-162-0	£9.99	Aug
Glasgow (pb)	1-85937-190-6	£9.99	Aug
Hertfordshire (pb)	1-85937-247-3	£9.99	Aug
North London	1-85937-206-6	£14.99	Aug
Victorian & Edwardian Maritime Album	1-85937-144-2	£17.99	Aug
Victorian Seaside	1-85937-159-0	£17.99	Aug
Cornish Coast	1-85937-163-9	£14.99	Sep
County Durham	1-85937-123-x	£14.99	Sep
Dorset Living Memories	1-85937-210-4	£14.99	Sep
Herefordshire	1-85937-174-4	£14.99	Sep
Kent Living Memories	1-85937-125-6	£14.99	Sep
Leeds (pb)	1-85937-202-3	£9.99	Sep
Ludlow (pb)	1-85937-176-0	£9.99	Sep
Norfolk (pb)	1-85937-195-7	£9.99	Sep
Somerset	1-85937-153-1	£14.99	Sep
Tees Valley & Cleveland	1-85937-211-2	£14.99	Sep
Thanet (pb)	1-85937-116-7	£9.99	Sep
Tiverton (pb)	1-85937-178-7	£9.99	Sep
Victorian and Edwardian Sussex	1-85937-157-4	£14.99	Sep
Weymouth (pb)	1-85937-209-0	£9.99	Sep
Worcestershire	1-85937-152-3	£14.99	Sep
Yorkshire Living Memories	1-85937-166-3	£14.99	Sep
British Life A Century Ago (pb)	1-85937-213-9	£9.99	Oct
Camberley (pb)	1-85937-222-8	£9.99	Oct
Cardiff (pb)	1-85937-093-4	£9.99	Oct
Carmarthenshire	1-85937-216-3	£14.99	Oct
Cornwall (pb)	1-85937-229-5	£9.99	Oct
English Country Houses	1-85937-161-2	£17.99	Oct
Gloucestershire	1-85937-102-7	£14.99	Oct
Humberside	1-85937-215-5	£14.99	Oct
Manchester (pb)	1-85937-198-1	£9.99	Oct
Middlesex	1-85937-158-2	£14.99	Oct
Norfolk Living Memories	1-85937-217-1	£14.99	Oct
Preston (pb)	1-85937-212-0	£9.99	Oct
South Hams	1-85937-220-1	£14.99	Oct
Suffolk	1-85937-221-x	£9.99	Oct
Swansea (pb)	1-85937-167-1	£9.99	Oct
West Yorkshire (pb)	1-85937-201-5	£9.99	Oct

See Frith books on the internet www.frithbook.co.uk

FRITH PRODUCTS & SERVICES

Francis Frith would doubtless be pleased to know that the pioneering publishing venture he started in 1860 still continues today. A hundred and forty years later, The Francis Frith Collection continues in the same innovative tradition and is now one of the foremost publishers of vintage photographs in the world. Some of the current activities include:

Interior Decoration

Today Frith's photographs can be seen framed and as giant wall murals in thousands of pubs, restaurants, hotels, banks, retail stores and other public buildings throughout the country. In every case they enhance the unique local atmosphere of the places they depict and provide reminders of gentler days in an increasingly busy and frenetic world.

Product Promotions

Frith products are used by many major companies to promote the sales of their own products or to reinforce their own history and heritage. Frith promotions have been used by Hovis bread, Courage beers, Scots Porage Oats, Colman's mustard, Cadbury's foods, Mellow Birds coffee, Dunhill pipe tobacco, Guinness, and Bulmer's Cider.

Genealogy and Family History

As the interest in family history and roots grows world-wide, more and more people are turning to Frith's photographs of Great Britain for images of the towns, villages and streets where their ancestors lived; and, of course, photographs of the churches and chapels where their ancestors were christened, married and buried are an essential part of every genealogy tree and family album.

Frith Products

All Frith photographs are available Framed or just as Mounted Prints and Posters (size 23 x 16 inches). These may be ordered from the address below. From time to time other products - Address Books, Calendars, Table Mats, etc - are available.

The Internet

Already twenty thousand Frith photographs can be viewed and purchased on the internet. By the end of the year 2000 some 60,000 Frith photographs will be available on the internet. The number of sites is constantly expanding, each focussing on different products and services from the Collection.
The main Frith sites are listed below.
www.francisfrith.co.uk
www.frithbook.co.uk

See the complete list of Frith Books at:
www.frithbook.co.uk

This web site is regularly updated with the latest list of publications from the Frith Book Company. If you wish to buy books relating to another part of the country that your local bookshop does not stock, you may purchase on-line.

For further information, trade, or author enquiries please contact us at the address below:
The Francis Frith Collection, Frith's Barn, Teffont, Salisbury, Wiltshire, England SP3 5QP.
Tel: +44 (0)1722 716 376 Fax: +44 (0)1722 716 881 Email: uksales@francisfrith.com

See Frith books on the internet www.frithbook.co.uk

TO RECEIVE YOUR FREE MOUNTED PRINT

Mounted Print
Overall size 14 x 11 inches

Cut out this Voucher and return it with your remittance for £1.50 to cover postage and handling, to UK addresses. For overseas addresses please include £4.00 post and handling. Choose any photograph included in this book. Your SEPIA print will be A4 in size, and mounted in a cream mount with burgundy rule lines, overall size 14 x 11 inches.

Order additional Mounted Prints at HALF PRICE (only £7.49 each*)
If there are further pictures you would like to order, possibly as gifts for friends and family, purchase them at half price (no additional postage and handling required).

Have your Mounted Prints framed*
For an additional £14.95 per print you can have your chosen Mounted Print framed in an elegant polished wood and gilt moulding, overall size 16 x 13 inches (no additional postage and handling required).

---
* IMPORTANT!
These special prices are only available if ordered using the original voucher on this page (no copies permitted) and at the same time as your free Mounted Print, for delivery to the same address
---

Frith Collectors' Guild

From time to time we publish a magazine of news and stories about Frith photographs and further special offers of Frith products. If you would like 12 months FREE membership, please return this form.

Send completed forms to:
The Francis Frith Collection, Frith's Barn, Teffont, Salisbury, Wiltshire SP3 5QP

Voucher for **FREE** and Reduced Price Frith Prints

Picture no.	Page number	Qty	Mounted @ £7.49	Framed + £14.95	Total Cost
		1	Free of charge*	£	£
			£7.49	£	£
			£7.49	£	£
			£7.49	£	£
			£7.49	£	£
			£7.49	£	£

Please allow 28 days for delivery	* **Post & handling**	£1.50
Book Title	**Total Order Cost**	£

Please do not photocopy this voucher. Only the original is valid, so please cut it out and return it to us.

I enclose a cheque / postal order for £ ....
made payable to 'The Francis Frith Collection'
OR please debit my Mastercard / Visa / Switch / Amex card
Number ....
Issue No (Switch only) .... Valid from (Amex/Switch) ....
Expires .... Signature ....
Name Mr/Mrs/Ms ....
Address ....
....
....
.... Postcode ....
Daytime Tel No .... Valid to 31/12/02

The Francis Frith Collectors' Guild
Please enrol me as a member for 12 months free of charge.

Name Mr/Mrs/Ms ....
Address ....
....
....
.... Postcode ....

Free Print - see overleaf